Spiritual
Metamorphosis
Volume 1

Spiritual Metamorphosis Volume 1

Gate by Gate

Ralph Riley

This publication is meant as a source of valuable information for the reader, however it is not meant as a substitute for direct expert assistance. If such level of assistance is required, the services of a competent professional should be sought.

Copyright © 2023 by Ralph Riley

All rights reserved. No part of this book may be reproduced or transmitted in any form or by any means, electronic or mechanical, including photocopying, recording, or any information storage and retrieval system, without permission in writing from the author.

ISBN: 978-1-6653-0579-2 - Paperback
eISBN: 978-1-6653-0580-8 - ePub

These ISBNs are the property of BookLogix for the express purpose of sales and distribution of this title. The content of this book is the property of the copyright holder only. BookLogix does not hold any ownership of the content of this book and is not liable in any way for the materials contained within. The views and opinions expressed in this book are the property of the Author/Copyright holder, and do not necessarily reflect those of BookLogix.

Library of Congress Control Number: 2023906638

∞This paper meets the requirements of ANSI/NISO Z39.48-1992 (Permanence of Paper)

Scripture quotations are taken from the Holy Bible, King James Version (Public Domain).

051723

I dedicate this book to Mr. Kenneth Riley, my brother and brother in Christ. It is his obedience to the effectual calling of God that the gospel of Jesus Christ was preached and my pricked heart received the gift of faith that has brought me to this place. The "Word of Faith" ministry opened the Sheep Gate door, where I began my spiritual metamorphosis. I'm forever grateful, my brother.

Contents

Introduction	ix

Chapter 1: Embryo Phase	**1**
Why I Must Be Born Again?	1
How Do I Get Born Again?	5
Spiritual Growth	11
Sheep Gate (Salvation)	12
Application	15
Summary	16

Chapter 2: Larva Phase	**19**
Eat and Grow Spiritually	19
Bread of Life	20
The Host Plant	25
Spiritual Growth	28
Fish Gate (Evangelize)	28
Application	30
Old Gate (Foundational)	31
Application	32
Summary	33

Chapter 3: Pupation Phase	**35**
Captivity Designed by God	37
Dying to Self	39
Breaking Up Fallow Ground	42
Renewed Nature	46
Spiritual Growth	48

The Valley Gate (Baptism by Fire)	49
Application	63
The Dung Gate (Deny Self)	63
Application	74
The Fountain Gate (Filled Spirit)	75
Application	82
Acknowledgments	*83*

Introduction

Growing up in a small town in Florida with dirt roads and churches on every corner may seem boring and lifeless, but I wouldn't change a thing from my journey. This was a time when less was more, and the precious commodity called "time" was spent with family, going to church, and participating in the many church programs, school activities, sports, and escaping the pressure to "keep up with the Joneses" by conforming to the fashion of the world by way of shopping malls, liquor stores, etc. A time when purpose and passion were found in the advantage of life that produced the fruits of good character and moral beliefs unconsciously. These standards, handed down from generations, are not the final story but acted as an apparatus until the calling of God was at hand and the renewing of the mind with God's word could take place. A time when family, friends, and the neighborhood had deep concerns about the character, activity, behavior, and future of others. The church performed responsibilities as the safe haven and the only holy place we knew. A time when the neighborhood praised others with good reports, cared for the souls of the neighborhood, and resourced excellence in those who demonstrated the zeal and fortitude to advance their future.

I can still hear the voice of my mother as she uttered the words, "God always has a ram tied in the bush," as she relinquished her last dime to resource my fleshly desires. I knew not what she meant, and my flesh didn't care. My mother's compassion and warm heart needed not to be taken advantage of; she just rather you be equipped to fulfill your heart's desires rather than to prepare for daily life essentials.

I began writing this book in 2009 and was derailed time and time again until there was some self-evidence in my life that I could express the parallel of the caterpillar to a butterfly and the born-again babe in Christ to a mature believer. Believers who have taken on the ministry of reconciliation to make disciples of Jesus Christ. Believers who have been through the fire of the Valley Gate, experienced the filling of the Holy Spirit in the Fountain Gate, and now rest, awaiting Jesus's return.

Having been fascinated with butterflies and their unbelievable beauty, I was drawn to the metamorphosis process. Neither did I know God would provide insight (revelation knowledge) regarding the parallel between the metamorphosis of the caterpillar to the butterfly and the born-again babe in Christ.

God's purpose for believers is connected to believers completing the metamorphosis process by being molded in the image of his Son Jesus Christ.

The word of God commands believers to be

transformed—not adding to one's religious devotion or one's spiritual rituals; not providing a better version of oneself, which is no change but starting anew (change in nature). God has instructed believers to be transformed by renewing their minds to the rules, laws, regulations, and culture of the Kingdom of God (God's way of doing things).

God has directed and commanded believers to enroll in the metamorphosis process to offer their bodies as living sacrifices. This metamorphosis is required to experience all that Jesus accomplished on the cross and prepare believers to be fitting, holy, and acceptable to God.

Surely, we are living in a time where the world and its systems have failed mankind, and the fabric of what we believed and how we lived in our sinful nature (fleshly, carnal minds) does not provide the character and mindset to accomplish the call of God for our lives. God's plan to restore man is going to be executed through the body of Christ and those willing to complete the metamorphosis process, for reproduction purposes, are equipped and favored by God to accomplish his great commission.

Believers' desire to be changed and receive a greater degree of the glory of God will be revealed in the metamorphosis process. Only through metamorphosis can we as believers engage in spiritual growth and complete our course designed by the living God.

Believers' confession of sin is not enough to empower the believers to walk in the Spirit of God nor prepare believers to yield themselves as living sacrifices. God's command to be transformed is better identified in the complete metamorphosis process.

God's plan to reconcile the world through Jesus Christ and his ambassadors hinges on avoiding being conformed or fashioned to this world and its system. God's plan to restore mankind is going to be exercised through the church and those willing to complete the metamorphosis acting as true witnesses matured to the phase of adulthood; capable of reproducing sons of God empowered to cause change with signs and wonders following them.

Without metamorphosis, there is little or no demonstration of God's presence or knowledge on this earth. Without metamorphosis, believers will continue to reproduce a nature unable to change or move from sanctification (set apart for God's purpose) to glorification (praise and worshipping God), reproducing incompletely transformed believers with no likeness of Christ. Without complete metamorphosis, believers cannot be trusted or empowered with the deep things of God and will struggle to become the Amen, or the confirmation of the word of God.

The indwelling spirit will not force believers to obey the commandments of God; he will not strengthen the believer's faith without a relationship with Christ.

The call to be transformed—to activate the new creature as old things are passed away, to put away the old, fleshy nature, and be transformed into a nature designed by God—will fill the void in mankind's spirit that only God can fill. No matter what your social position, title, background, or economic status, we all must be transformed by renewing our minds. Anything short of the completion of this transformation and we forfeit God's given talents and purpose to expand the Kingdom of God.

Our mission, as believers, to preach and teach the gospel will be difficult if we fail to complete the metamorphosis of receiving the Oath of Commission through a Pentecost understanding. Our commission is to extend God's Kingdom from heaven to earth through our spirit as we dominate the earth as living sacrifices tried and proven to manifest his divine nature through our bodies. The people of this world are waiting on the sons and daughters of God to manifest God's promises and display his awesome light.

The intent of this book is to minister the need to complete the transformation, providing God the Creator with a living sacrifice for the expansion of the

Kingdom of God where Jesus Christ is the King, and his word is final.

This book is designed to provide:

- a visual of the transformation of a believer's development process as it parallels the butterfly metamorphosis process;
- to provide a processing map for believers to identify what phase of the metamorphosis has been completed in their lives and how much is required to reach spiritual adulthood;
- to set up a developmental process for transformation by renewing one's mind and identifying themselves through the fruit of the Holy Spirit.

The book of Nehemiah provides a processing map for spiritual growth. The order in which the builder began the process, architects set forth an order in which the gates to the temple, and the details regarding each gate, can be used as a spiritual metaphor describing the believer's spiritual growth. These gates and the repair of the wall of Jerusalem can be found in the book of Nehemiah 3.

Spiritual Metamorphosis Volume 1

The metamorphosis is to change one's spiritual nature. This book will use the process of the caterpillar to the butterfly to provide a process map regarding a believer's spiritual growth in each phase of the butterfly transformation. This book will also use Nehemiah's gates to help identify one's spiritual development based on the fruits and gifts of the Holy Spirit.

Simply put, this book is designed to identify yourself in the complete metamorphosis phase (spiritual development) and build you up with encouraging truths. As you read this book, I urge you to get to know your heavenly Father with the purpose of completing the transformation for the expansion of the Kingdom of God, with the urgency to dedicate yourself to the cause of these efforts and the course set before you.

Solomon, the son of David, the wisest man on earth prior to Jesus's arrival in the flesh, wrote, "Everything is nothing if everything under the sun is all it is. All is vanity." The world takes away the imagination of man and limits his or her ability to see the unseen, to experience the Kingdom of God. Solomon wrote all is vanity under the sun apart from God's purpose and his plan for your life. The world has handed humanity a false standard to seek and worship the creation (things that are temporal) and ignore the creator (things that are eternal).

Leonard Woolf, a successful author, recipient of

numerous awards, achiever of financial success of millions of dollars received from his work, and favored by men all over the world, wrote, "I see clearly that I have achieved practically nothing." Apart from God, there is no point to life, there is no profit to life.

This change in the nature process allows believers to be transported (brought out of darkness) and transcended (surpass fleshly limitation) from the powers and authority that once governed mankind's thought process (regeneration spirit) so that they may begin living according to the Kingdom of God free from desolation, poverty, sickness, and sin.

Chapter 1

Embryo Phase

> *The adult butterfly (complete metamorphosis) continues its existence by mating (reproducing) and laying eggs. Caterpillars (butterfly larvae) hatch from these eggs to begin the metamorphosis process. The eggs are laid near the food plant(s) that will be used by the caterpillar for development.*

Likewise, Jesus is the firstborn from the dead. He is the self-replicating substance that carries the spiritual genetic information for a divine nature. Jesus (word of God) is the unchangeable requirement for reproducing himself to continue his existence (purpose) on earth until he returns. This nature includes the fundamental and distinctive characteristics (image and likeness) of God himself.

Why I Must Be Born Again?

This book's objectives are not to highlight and provide an in-depth salvation message for unbelievers. The intent of this book, as mentioned in the introduction, is to present a spiritual-growth processing map for believers to identify where they are in their transformation process.

However, I can't just assume all readers of this book have an understanding of why one must be born again as a prerequisite to begin the metamorphosis process.

The Bible said you must be born again to experience the Kingdom of God (God's way of doing business). God is advocating a renewed spirit to resume and reestablish (restore) a relationship with him for self-identification and purpose. Mankind's spirit was interrupted at a natural birth, is spiritually dead, and will require regeneration by the creator of all things (God the Father). This regeneration of mankind's spirit will lend itself to the regrowth of any damage occurred while operating in the sinful nature and return mankind's spirit to its original spiritual intent and purpose.

It is vital that mankind comes to the knowledge of God the Father to rekindle a relationship with Him and save their soul. Mankind was born with a sinful nature, at no fault of his or her own, and was born into this world as a spiritual orphan; one who has deprived their heritage, benefits, and privileges of spiritual birthrights due to the death (separation) of their spiritual Father; one without the nourishment, protection, and guidance of God the Father; one who is born from a seed with no identity with the nature of the man

Adam disconnected from God—a man deprived from a spiritual example to follow; living from the outside inwardly. Spiritual metamorphosis is the process to move the babe in Christ to adulthood, identifying with God the Father, no longer a spiritual orphan.

The spirit of man at natural birth operates in a hypnotic state, or a state of rest under the influence of a sinful nature. A nature with no authority or freedom to say no to sin; no authority to influence one's behavior, character, reaction to life challenges, nor the temptation and desires of the flesh.

Likewise, in the spiritual realm, an unregenerated spiritual being, not having the knowledge of its spiritual Father nor having the capability to spend time with God, leaves mankind puzzled regarding one's identity and creates a gap (breach, crevice) between mankind and his spiritual Father.

This gap, or the broken communication link, will leave mankind as an orphan (separated from their creator or spiritual Father)—having no spiritual understanding of their purpose, inheritance, whereabouts, bloodline, and all that God the Father has prepared for them. God's purpose and plan for mankind have not changed. If we look closely, we all have been under tutors and governed by people in our lives to bring us to a place where we need someone or something the world couldn't offer.

Having been bound by our fleshly desires, we obey

the god of this world (Satan), unconsciously, because of an unregenerate spirit and sinful nature.

This rekindled relationship with God will reveal the purpose and plan for a believer's life and cause one to identify themselves with God the Father through faith in Jesus Christ by the Holy Spirit. Mankind's purpose, and mere existence, is connected to having a relationship with Jesus Christ by faith, causing one to be free from the penalty of sins (old and new). This takes away the stony heart (wicked heart) out of one's flesh and gives them a heart of flesh (causing one to love).

If mankind is going to have a relationship with God the Father, the creator of all things, and experience or witness the Kingdom of God (God's constitutional rights for those that believe), being born again is not optional. The word of God declares that God is holy and mankind's heart at birth is wicked. Because of God's holiness, sin separates mankind from God. Being born again provides a regenerated (recreate, reestablish, reawaken, restore) spirit, bringing a believer into a new life, regaining hope for an eternal life no longer without God and no longer a stranger to the covenant of God's promises. This regeneration is an activation and restoration of mankind's spirit with the capability to receive spiritual things. A regenerated spirit provides an avenue by which mankind can commune with a Holy God and receive spiritual truths to change one's life and the lives of others God has put in their care. This spiritual regeneration is an unimaginable experience that cannot be told in its fullness.

Man, in his unregenerate state, knows and by "the spirit of man," which is in him. If I have the will to know certain scientific facts, by my human spirit, I'm enabled to investigate, think, and weigh the evidence. If I set myself to the task, I may become a world-renowned scientist of great accomplishment.

However, my human spirit is "limited to the things of God." If I want to know about the things of God, my unregenerated spirit will *not* be able to know them. If mankind wants to know why they exist—or if man wants to know what their purpose in being born again to meet and greet God is—the Father is required.

At the end of the day, when all standards and definitions of the world's success are accomplished, the void in the heart of mankind remains.

How Do I Get Born Again?

This is an interesting question asked by many. My feeble attempt to explain this spiritual out-of-body experience may or may not provide the comfort or satisfaction that will put one's spirit at ease.

As mentioned previously, this book is not a salvation message. After much pondering and praying to give me the answer to this question, "How do I get born again?" I could only acknowledge there isn't one. Because this is a personal, intimate relationship with Christ, there is no set pattern or protocol. Our heavenly Father is more than able to meet you where you are and speak to you within their ability to hear or provide spiritual ears to hear spiritual things. Because of God's love for mankind, he makes no distinction between the haves and the have-nots. God is no respecter of persons; it is his will that all come to the knowledge of him and experience an unconditional love only he can unveil.

It would be mentally deranged for me to just say, "Receive the Lord Jesus Christ as your Lord and Savior and begin believing in him, trusting in him, and he will show himself strong."

Therefore, I will provide my story (summary) as everyone has their own. This intimate relationship with Christ covers all facets of intimacy in my journey, which includes experimental intimacy (spiritual) during daily activities, leaving me unsure and unable to explain the love, peace, and serenity of an alienated force. The audible voice of the loving Father kept me up at night at that time, praying for understanding and some logical solution to this encounter. I thank God for my parents who taught their children to pray and ask God the Father for answers. I recalled the many bedtime stories of my parents, how our heavenly Father had brought them thus far and how they had no options or resources to feed their family without the grace and blessing of God. It was prayer that got them through the tough times, so I knew to pray. Because, at this time, I had no relationship with Christ, I didn't know my God. I only knew about him through church messages, friends, family members, etc. Although I had no relationship and no capacity to have a relationship with God, he loved me and showed a strong presence in my daily activities from sunup to sundown.

A relationship with God is formed through the knowledge of his existence by hearing the living words spoken to the believer's ears with the influence of God's ability that will cause an unregenerated spirit to ponder an unfamiliar presence. God's presence will press upon you with a love that draws mankind. A love that causes the spirit of man to seek understanding; to thirst for a deeper love outside of physical attributes; a love that touches the very essence and splendor of mankind; a love openly present in one's life through familiar circumstance and daily activities. God will meet you where you are in this world. God is all-knowing and foreknew you before the foundation of the world.

When I'm experiencing emotional intimacy with like-minded believers, it allows me to share my feelings and shortcomings with others in a safety net without the fear of judgment. This is a mutual vulnerability between others who have experienced similar encounters. An intimacy, although uncomfortable, provides a feeling of belonging—no longer isolated or alienated from spiritual expressions in religious circles and activities. Being able to relate to one's emotional outburst, sharing tears of happiness, and shouting as the word of God is fulfilled in our lives is truly a blessing.

This physical intimacy was more than the trees in the forest, the rising and setting of the sun, more than the midnight moon setting, more than the stars strategically placed in the heavens—it is a pure demonstration of God's intimate presence in my life.

During this time, God the Father was drawing me closer with a demonstration of his love of constant communion and a constant presence that couldn't be articulated. He began to speak to me through everything visible and every walk of life propelled me to want to know more that had escaped me for years.

Many years before I received the Lord Jesus Christ in my heart (born again) there was a pricking (penetrating) of my spirit by God that provided me the will to fill an emptiness in my life that couldn't be explained. Something was missing, regardless of worldly accomplishments. Accomplishments weren't enough and had no value outside of the bragging rights in appropriate conversations and circles. The more I heard the word of God and wanted to understand this love, the more God pressed upon me through his love and demonstrated his very existence through an unexplainable presence. There was a close presence of God in my life while he gave me the will to seek him.

Let me try to explain: The world didn't change, but my perspective of things surrounding my daily activities did. How I once viewed things from an educational or experienced standpoint, now had a new perspective based on the word of God:

- the many late-night visitations from a spiritual God, having a disembodied (spiritual) experience;
- the many signs of God, once ignored, are now amplified;
- the many people God placed in my life to let me know God the Father is seeking my attention;
- the many isolated places I found myself with no one to call on but God;
- the many gifts (biblical books and bibles) from benefactors and midwives God places in my life;
- God's constant presence and protection from the arms of this world;
- unexplainable long walks at night asking God to show himself strong in my life.

Again, this is just a summary of my story. I would love to take the credit for my journey, but it is God who gave me the desire and the will to want more of this love that had found me.

Then, there came a time when the world's system began to show itself worthless, and regardless of the world's definition of success, it wasn't enough. There was yet a void that remained unfilled to satisfy my hunger and thirst for a love I didn't know. It was the will of God and his love for me that brought me out of darkness (to see what I could not see before) and fill my emptiness with love for others through his word. It was God who pressed upon me a need for a change in my mind (repent). God chose me, I didn't choose him.

One certain Sunday morning, after many attempts to ask Jesus the Son of God to come into my life and be my Lord and Savior—after many restless nights of recording my sinful past, after fighting the enemy in my own strength, losing the battle time and time again—God stepped in and gave me the power to stand up and unconsciously move to the front of the church and ask Jesus to come into my life.

One will need to be drawn by God the Father through love. One who has heard the gospel and believed that God loves them. No one can come to Jesus unless God the Father draws them (giving him the desire to come). None of being born again is based on your desires, your will, but it's God working in you the will to do. The unregenerated spirit of mankind is fully aware of one's sinful nature, driven by fleshly desires and the things of this world that try to fill a spiritual void only the Spirit of God can satisfy. This void of not knowing who I was as a spiritual orphan frightened me and propelled me to repent and believe the gospel of Jesus Christ. The decision to want more out of life, to fill the void that the things of this world couldn't, and to provide a calculated or expected end to life, has brought me to this book.

It is my hope and prayer that this book prepares an invitation to all of mankind to enter the Sheep Gate, the place of sacrifice for atonement for the sins of the people.

Spiritual Growth

Have you accepted the Effectual Calling?

In each phase of the metamorphosis of the caterpillar to the butterfly and the parallel of the believer, each gate will tell a story. This processing map will assist the believer to identify where they are in their spiritual growth process in the metamorphosis. As mentioned in the introduction, this spiritual-growth processing map is designed to challenge the believer's whereabouts in the metamorphosis process.

The Embryo Phase of the spiritual metamorphosis consists of the Sheep Gate, where the believer has accepted the effectual calling (successful in receiving a desire or intent) of God.

Sheep Gate (Salvation)

The first gate in the rebuild of the tabernacle in Jerusalem (a place by which God can reside) is the Sheep Gate. This gate was used to bring in animals to be sacrificed for the sins of mankind. This is the only gate by which mankind can be saved and have a relationship with their spiritual Father. This is the gate by which Jesus is the only way to God, by God's grace through faith in Jesus Christ.

The Sheep Gate is the only gate consecrated (set apart as holy), the only gate after rebuilding. The builders did not place bolts and locks to ensure all who desire have a right by the grace of God to enter in and get to know their spiritual Father. This is an effort to show forth his grace, presence, and power in this world and the world to come. This gift of life allows mankind to have a relationship with God the Father and act on his behalf as workmanship to further his Kingdom. This is an opportunity to put away the bondage, sickness, poverty, and all the enemy's tricks to kill, steal, and destroy mankind. This gate provides a safety net (hedges) camped all around the believer until the complete metamorphosis can be accomplished or until Jesus returns for his church.

A believer's spiritual-growth processing map begins with the Sheep Gate as Jesus is the way, the truth, and the life. It is by God's grace salvation is made available through faith in Jesus Christ. After believers have been touched by God through his word and received some spiritual understanding (calling), mankind can take full advantage of the grace, mercy, and gift of God. Mankind can enter the Sheep Gate and receive Jesus Christ as their personal Savior. *Being born again provides a regenerated (recreated, reestablished, reawakened, restored) spirit, bringing a believer into a new life and regaining hope as previously mentioned.* This is the gate whereby the power and presence of God fill a void in mankind's spirit that only he can. This is the gate whereby the believers are born again from on high, old things are passed away, and all things become new.

The entry door to the Sheep Gate is Jesus the Christ. This door is the only door to enter into the sheepfold, whereby the sheep (those with a regenerated spirit) can hear the voice of the shepherd for salvation and be delivered from the bondage of this dark world. There is no other door by which mankind can enter the sheepfold of the shepherd Jesus Christ. He is the propitiation (ransom) for the sins of mankind.

The Sheep Gate Experience

The Sheep Gate experience is where the born-again (afresh) believers began to experience a love from

God that's more real than any earthly presence. This relationship began in prayer, and God's constant presence throughout the day is fitting for spiritual development. The Sheep Gate experience is getting to know yourself through:

- the lens of God as he reveals himself through his word (scripture);
- life experience in your favor;
- late-night conversations with a God you can't see in the natural world but communicate with in the spiritual realm;
- a spiritual discernment activated to avoid harmful traps of the enemy, to see the end state of a decision as if you foreknew the outcome.

This relationship with God through Christ identifies believers who have the kind of faith that speaks confidently about who God is and his impact on their life. This relationship with God provides a boldness to speak with assurance that God loves them with unconditional love (agape love; love unlimited; selfless love).

In the Sheep Gate, believers began to use the word "saved," knowing that God is real and his love and presence is real. Believers understand they are saved from their past, present, and future sinful acts and their consequences. They have been justified by Christ's death and resurrection. Believers understand this strange, unexplainable relationship is more than just words of exaltation or some religious expression of emotions, but a relationship between a loving spiritual Father and son or daughter. Believers began to experience their salvation with a constant reminder of who they are in Christ escaping the trials, tribulation, and condemnation in this world that once rid them of their joy and peace. Believers experience spiritual blessings (favor, revelation, knowledge), performing great exploits through the knowledge of God's grace, promises, love, and attributes, and the spoils of the victory of his death, burial, and resurrection.

Application

Jesus Christ is the only one who can save (do away with the penalty of sin) mankind. It is through his obedience, his sacrifice, and his faithfulness that the believer's sin is washed away. Without the blood of Jesus Christ, mankind has no life in them.

If you haven't decided to ask Jesus to come into your life, please do so immediately. No one knows the day or the hour of Jesus's return to his church. Jesus is the door to the Sheep Gate, where God can restore mankind to their original status. Please enter the Sheep Gate and experience Jesus Christ for yourself. You don't have to go before the church (building) and pastor to receive Jesus as your Lord and Savior. If you experienced the love of God (God's calling) expressed through unexplainable events, and you have heard the good news that Jesus is alive, change your posture (go to your knees), and pray a simple prayer, asking Jesus, who is alive, to come into your life and save you.

Summary

Surely, we live in a time where the world and its system have failed us and the fabric of what we believe through the flesh and carnal mind cannot provide victory over the stress and wickedness in this world and its system(s).

It is vital that mankind comes to the knowledge of God the Father to rekindle a relationship with God and save one's soul. Mankind was born with a sinful nature at no fault of their own and were born into this world as a spiritual orphan. If mankind wants to know the truth of the matter pertaining to salvation and deliverance, being born again is not optional.

Being born again provides:

- a regenerated spirit delivering the believer(s) from the power of darkness;
- redeeming the believer through the blood of Jesus;
- forgiving the believer of their sins;
- transfering the believer into the Kingdom of Jesus Christ.

Jesus is the way, the truth, and the life—no man can see the Kingdom of God without him. Mankind can do nothing without Jesus Christ. It is through the knowledge of Jesus Christ that believers are no longer unfruitful and barren in the Kingdom of God.

Phycologist studies have demonstrated that the human mind operates in the conscious mindset (reasoning, judgment, emotions, protection, critical thinking, will power, and planning), accounting for approximately 12 percent of our daily activities, 12 percent of our reaction to stress and pressure presented by this world daily, and 12 percent of the decision-making process that governs our lives. An unregenerated spirit's character and conduct are a result of an unconscious mindset (the body's reaction) at an alarming 80-plus percent of mankind's daily activities.

Consider these numbers with an understanding that mankind is born into this world separated from God (no hope), with a mindset filled with evil thoughts and depravity through physical birth that cannot be told in its fullness. Mankind begat itself. Our children are suffering because believers failed to complete the metamorphosis. Our children and neighborhood lack prototypes and examples to follow. The depravity embedded at birth and the lack of spiritual involvement continues to reign in the lives of those who are seeking the sons and daughters of God for help.

If we as believers operate in the unconscious without completing the spiritual metamorphosis, our behavior and reaction to the challenges of the enemy's plot will leave us vulnerable at the alarming rate of 88 percent of our daily activities. Believers will be subjected to being devoured by the enemy, never reaching their full potential in Christ. I thank my God for his Grace and mercy that fills the gap of separation from him until spiritual development can be accomplished—until complete metamorphosis is evident of God's presence in the believer's lifestyle—and walk with Jesus.

Chapter 2

Larva Phase

Eat and Grow Spiritually

> *The caterpillar begins its life in a food source designed for its metamorphosis, a nature filled with no characteristics of its adulthood. After hatching in the appropriate food source, the caterpillar begins to eat and grow. The caterpillars feed on specific host plants, which can range from a single species to many different species. The food source for the caterpillar is selected and chosen by the creator of all things. The adult butterfly will lay the egg(s) of the caterpillar in their food source designed for growth, purpose, habitation, image, and the glory of God. Each species of butterfly has specific host plants on which the adult butterflies lay their eggs.*

In this chapter, we will parallel the caterpillar metamorphosis to a butterfly and the new birth of the believer. This metaphor will highlight the parallel in a spiritual allegory (hidden or ulterior meaning) versus the physical metamorphosis of the caterpillar to the butterfly.

Likewise, as the caterpillar begins its life in a designed food source, the born-again believer is positioned in the body of Christ (the host plant) until spiritual growth can take place. The word of God is the only food source for spiritual growth as mankind cannot live by bread alone, but by every word out of the mouth of God. The purpose of the larva phase for the believer is to eat (meditate on) the word of God and grow spiritually. The newborn believer is driven by the love of God to study the word of God so that they might do the pleasing things in God's sight, that they might know him.

The Larva Phase of the metamorphosis is where the word of God (food source) will establish a spiritual relationship with God and strengthen the believer's faith and hope while they're camouflaged in Christ.

Bread of Life

We Are What We Eat

As believers, God has prepared a food source fit for spiritual metamorphosis from a sinful nature to a divine nature. A believer's food source is not physical but spiritual and fitting for edifying a believer's thought process. It is the word of God that will enable a believer's metamorphosis to grow spiritually, building a prayer, praise, and worship lifestyle.

This is the starting point where believers will eat and grow, empowering them to cultivate, influence, and colonize all that God has planned for the believer's life.

The bread of life is a precious commodity and requires teaching at a level of understanding as babes in Christ require the milk of the word of God. Babes in Christ will receive the bread of life in their eyes of understanding and the phase of their metamorphosis. The Larva Phase requires the babes in Christ to receive the first oracles of the principles of God (faith toward God, doctrine of baptism, resurrection of the dead, eternal judgment, foundation of repentance from dead works). Babes in Christ are unskillful in the word of righteousness and not apt to understand nor appreciate the deeper aspects of God's promises, nor what they contain. If the babe in Christ follows the modern-day trend to worship at the local ministry (church), spiritual growth may be hindered or delayed. This bread of life (milk of the word) is a food source that can be digested by babes in Christ to further their faith. This milk nurses immature believers to undergo spiritual development and build trust and confidence in the word of God.

The food source designed for the physical body will

cause growth that maintains mankind's health while living in this world, but will not meet the requirements for change in nature or eternal life. Believers, and those that follow Christ, will be afforded a food source that will cause a spiritual change. This spiritual maturity will result in developing disciples in the likeness of Christ. It is the revealing of the word of God that will transform believers from a sinful nature to a divine nature. This is the food source that doesn't cause physical obesity. This bread of life is required for complete metamorphosis, acting as the anchor to the believer's walk with God to promote steadfastness. This food source cannot be ignored but must be embraced to cause a change in the believer's love for mankind. The meditation in this prescribed food source is an effort to fulfill the great commandment of God, to prepare the hinges (love for mankind) of this commandment for future spiritual growth, taking full advantage of the grace of God.

This food source is the living word of God; it's the only food source designed for spiritual growth. The living word of God can make dead thoughts alive and dead narratives of destruction provide earnest hope to rest in until the manifestation of the believer's faith is unfaltering.

God's presence will cause believers to hunger for spiritual nutrients that will cause a change in their lives and the lives of those God has placed in the believer's midst. There have been countless times my meditation in the word of God the Holy Spirit unlocked a mystery of a parable or an incomplete message received from the pulpit. Shortly thereafter, this wisdom, understanding, and counsel from my meditation were for someone else God had placed in my life. The believer's hunger for spiritual nutrients goes beyond self-approval unto God but reaches the cry of fellow saints and those that are lost.

The bread of life is a vital source for the early development of babes in Christ. This spiritual bread is not made with fleshly inclinations, free from salt, sugar, yeast, or gluten. This food source is spiritual growth, nutrient-dense, and easy to digest at the level of one's understanding through the work of the Holy Spirit.

This spiritual food source is:

- without preservatives;
- without outside sources;
- not made by the hands of man;
- an incorruptible seed that is organic in nature and is pure to its essence and splendor.

This living word of God is a discerner of the thoughts and intents of the heart that leads to holiness.

Mankind, in general, cannot survive, and cannot

maintain some level of earnest hope (promises of God) without a relationship with God and the spiritual food source designed to develop faith. The image of the food source (seed of Christ) results in the image of Christ fulfilling the commandment of God to be Christ-minded in all that believers do. To be Christ-minded, believers no longer view the world through the lens of a sinful nature succumbing to its natural desires. Instead, believers must move away from their sinful nature at birth (denying temptations of the flesh) by living in accordance with the voice of the indwelling spirit.

The food source is also a protective form and a refuge from the enemy of this world. The more the seed of Christ (food source) is deposited in the believer's heart, the more they mimic the image of Jesus Christ. The word of God declares that we should be like him. This food source has unique identifiers (fruit of the Spirit of God) that demonstrate the presence and the power of God in the lives of believers.

This designed food source for the believer will provide nourishment essential for spiritual growth and maintenance (maintaining holiness, righteousness, etc.) for a spiritual walk with God. This food source is filled with ingredients that promote spiritual growth and provides energy (joy) to maintain life. It is in this food source that believers find the answers to the issues of life. The word of God is the pedigree of God's attributes, including omnipresence, omnipotence, and omniscience. The more believers eat the designed food source (living bread), the more life they have within them to say no to sin. The more this living bread is consumed, the more the image of Christ is demonstrated in our lives for others to witness the love and power of God.

The Host Plant

The caterpillars feed on specific host plants, which can range from a single species to many different species. Likewise, the believer will be directed to a host plant by the indwelling Holy Spirit.

A good host plant is steadfast, authentic to itself, and organic in its created form or nature. This *host plant* provided by the appropriate brook (ministry) invites and ushers the babe in Christ (born again) with open arms in the presence and love of God. Born-again believers may find a lack of spiritual nutrients in normal surroundings and will need to adhere to the voice of the Holy Spirit to go to the brook (ministry) suited for their spiritual development. God has provided provisions and a place of habitation for believers' spiritual growth through a *specific* host plant (ministry). The appropriate host plant will propel the believers' faith to be equipped to complete the course God set before them.

It is through this host plant that the unseen world

is revealed. This host plant is where believers developed ears to hear and eyes to see what couldn't be heard or seen before. The living bread received from the appropriate brook is digested in the believer's spirit to produce its own kind.

I'm reminded of the story of Elijah, when God caused a drought in the land of Gilead. God instructed his prophet Elijah to go to the Brook Cherith (a place of refuge beside the still waters), where Elijah would be fed manna (food source) from heaven. It was at this brook God had commanded the ravens to sustain Elijah with food and where the waters would be plentiful in a drought caused by God.

God has a plan for believers, the specific brook is the foundation and starting point for spiritual growth for the babe in Christ. This is the place where the first oracles of God are taught and received by babes in Christ.

I remember my experience as a babe in Christ, having received the indwelling Spirit of God and was excited about the Kingdom of God that put my soul to rest in Jesus Christ. I attended a ministry (church) because my family and friends attended it and the expectations to attend this church had great influence. The ministry of music was emotionally good, the church's format for service was familiar with my past, the service time was fitting for the Sunday football games on television, the distance to the church was comfortable, the congregation was religious folks, but the "love" expressed through hugging and kissing was not authenticated and my regenerated spirit did not agree (quenched at the call of the pastor to love on your neighbor). There came a time when this ministry could not provide the necessary spiritual nutrients that my regenerated spirit desired (thirst after).

A neighbor friend of mine attended another church and invited me to come and visit. After several conversations with this neighbor, after church services on Sundays and sometimes through the week, we communed talking about the word of God and God's plan for our lives. His level of understanding and zeal to share with me the gospel of Jesus Christ drew me to take advantage of his offer to come and visit their ministry. One Sunday, I decided to make the trip to their church, and the warm welcome received at the door by the ushers, and the congregation truly worshipped God in Spirit and truth (not entertaining), and the Spirit of God was present in this church. I had never experienced anything like this before. The message from the pulpit was edifying and food for thought. Near the end of the service, the church was asked to pray. As I begin to pray, an angel (messenger of God) placed their hands on my shoulders and began to pray with and for me.

She said, "God has a plan for your life, and you are

going to do great things in the Kingdom of God." I turned to say thank you and she quickly responded, "You don't need to turn to see who I am." So, I stopped and turned back to the front of the church. My soul was at rest in Christ and my spirit was filled with the Holy Spirit. My mind wondered who this angel (lady) was and why did she pray for a stranger? Only my neighbor knew me in this congregation.

I refer to this lady as an angel because I got a glance at her clothing color and wanted to give thanks for her prayers after service. Needless to say, she couldn't be found, yet she sat in the next row behind me. I search for her every Sunday with no results of her identity.

This church became my brook, where the word of God was presented in a matter in which I, as a babe in Christ, could hear and understand, see (experience) and receive the word of God.

Spiritual Growth

The Larva Phase of the spiritual metamorphosis consists of the Fish Gate and the Old Gate after believers have accepted the effectual calling (successful in receiving a desire or intent) of God.

Fish Gate (Evangelize)

The Fish Gate is where the fisherman brought in their catch of the day to sell to the fish market. The Fish Gate speaks to serve the Kingdom of God after being born again and receives Jesus as their personal Savior during the Sheep Gate. Salvation must precede service if the believer is going to be effective in the Kingdom of God, equipped with the indwelling Spirit of God. This is the gate where born-again believers express their love for God as neophytes as the word of God fills their hearts. This is the gate born-again believers spread the gospel based on the eyes of their understanding ("I was blind and now I see.").

The Fish Gate Experience

God wants to make believers into fishermen of men. For disciples to tell the story about Jesus the Christ, who has come as the means of believers' deliverance from sin (ransom). For disciples to tell the story that, because of his arrival, mankind can be reconciled to a spiritual Father.

Believers (fishermen), understanding the concept of fishing for fish, now use the same preparation, diligence, study, and research to save souls through the work of the Holy Spirit. Believers now cast their nets (gospel message) to reach mankind to tell the story. The same effort and risk to catch fish are now used to catch the hearts of mankind for the expansion of the Kingdom of God.

I remember my Fish Gate experience. Shortly after receiving Jesus Christ in my life, my narrative changed and all I could talk about was how Jesus came into my life and there was something inside of me that couldn't be explained in this phase of my life.

The message of the gospel of Jesus Christ is real. There was a burning fire on the inside of my regenerated spirit that caused (forced) me to share the good news with friends, family, and even strangers in public places. This fire filled my day and the desire to seek the word of God only grew stronger as God used this fire to reach others. I couldn't wait to tell everyone I knew that I was saved and Jesus Christ is the one who saved me. I couldn't wait to attend church and receive the word of God with pens and papers to write down every word that came out of the teacher's mouth. After receiving the word from the teacher, I would go home, review what I heard, and try to make some logical understanding of the message. This message (gospel) came not in words only, but in power so that I could see the unseen. I was blind and now could see things from a different perspective with knowledge and wisdom acquired through the voice of the indwelling Holy Spirit.

Application

Have you entered the Fish Gate (servicehood), or you are ashamed to tell those in your circle of life about Jesus Christ because of what they might say? Are you secretly seeking the Kingdom of God, only sharing the good news with people inside the walls of the church building? Are you serving the Lord as fishermen of men?

It's time to let go and let God. You hold the only antidote to your friends' and family's demise. The gospel of Jesus Christ is the power unto salvation (deliverance). Find a local church or ministry of the Holy Spirit's choosing and release yourself to the edifying of the church. God saved mankind to reach others. Believers are saved to serve.

Old Gate (Foundational)

The believer's spiritual-growth processing map continues in the Old Gate. The Old Gate can be discerned as the word of God has never changed. God created mankind to have a relationship with them. The message of the Old Gate is that God is the same yesterday and today and forever. There are no variables likely to change or shadows turning in him.

The Old Gate is the cornerstone as the word of God is timeless, organic, and consistent in the face of any circumstances or areas in one's life. Because the word of God never changes, it can be depended upon in times of need. Because God's love for mankind will never change, mankind can be changed.

The Old Gate Experience

The Old Gate is the starting of a new quarter (lodging in a specific place) that leads into the Valley Gate designed by God. This is the gate where believers are instructed to stand on the Old Path (the foundation of God's Grace) where God's love is expressed. God created man in his own image (Old Path) and likeness, and he is not ashamed of his creation. This is the gate where mankind walked in the cool day without fear. This is the good way, before sin existed. Believers walking in the Old Path describe godly living. God has not changed; he is the same God that created mankind to commune with them. The Old Path has always been faith and obedience. The "old folk" used the Old Gate saying without quoting the word of God. They would say things like, "What goes around comes around" or "If you don't have anything good to say, don't say anything at all."

Application

Have you found a place of rest for your soul? Have you found a place you can escape this dark world and find green pastures? Are you walking in the image and likeness of God (Old Path)? Have the words of faith and obedience filled your spirit for change?

I recommend trying the Old Gate, as it is God who first loved you. Believers serve a God that will always love them—a God that will never leave them nor forsake them. Jesus said, "Come unto me (walk with me) and I will give you rest." The conclusion of the will of God for mankind is to fear God and keep his commandments.

Summary

The Larva Phase is the place where believers begin to change their narrative (words of exhortation) as the Holy Spirit provides spiritual discernment to see the unseen grace of God in situations. We as believers miss God's opportunity to cause a change in our lives and the lives of others many times because we are too busy to consult the Holy Spirit for counsel. Without the counseling of the Holy Spirit, a believer's intellect will misdiagnose the cry for help.

Christ-minded believers are no longer strangers, alienated from a spiritual Father, who long to be in the presence of the believer. God's presence will enable believers to discern the things of God and his purpose, ignoring self-preservation to care and assist with empathy (when appropriate) for others.

Mankind's unregenerated spirit cannot receive the things of God, therefore leaving them vulnerable to the wiles of the god (Satan) of this world's destruction. Jesus's foretold coming as the gift of life was to:

- create an avenue by which to escape the depravities of the flesh;
- escape the very nature of physical birth through faith that Jesus Christ is the Son of God and the long-awaited Messiah (promised deliverer).

Jesus's sacrifice on the cross and resurrection paid the ransom for the sins of mankind, who is now appointed as the believer's High Priest.

Supernatural events have been arranged for those who obey the indwelling Spirit of God and find their food source and specific brook fitting for their spiritual growth. Believers are commanded to feast on the word of God continuously without ceasing.

Chapter 3

Pupation Phase
(Change in Nature)

In the complete metamorphosis of the caterpillar to the butterfly, the larva spins itself into a cocoon-like shell (captivity) to ensure an uninterrupted change in nature. The host plant (cleft of the rock) is the ideal place to begin the pupation phase, providing protection from the enemies of this world. This is the phase the caterpillar transitions into a butterfly, looking nothing like its prepupated state.

Likewise, believers will require a place of spiritual pupation (internal change) to ensure an uninterrupted change in nature. The host plant (cleft of the rock) from which the believer received their salvation is the ideal place for pupation, as the word of God is the seed for change. This place of pupation (captivity designed by God) will place the believer in a spiritual place, where their faith becomes unshakeable, and humility is inescapable.

The spiritual pupation place will challenge the believer's voice of what they evangelized in the Fish Gate and provide an experience with the Holy Spirit that will become the anchor of their soul. Most importantly, the change at this phase results in the believer being clothed in humility and obtaining the spiritual fruit (character and gifts of the Holy Spirit) required to complete the spiritual metamorphosis.

The Pupation Phase is the starting point of the metamorphosis for conversion of the believer's sinful nature to a divine nature designed by God. This Pupation Phase of the metamorphosis is where the believer desires to know the ways of God so that they might know the essence of who God is in their life.

This is the phase where a deeper relationship with God is needed for change. Getting to sit and commune with God in prayer, praise, and worship, in an uninterrupted space and time, is heavenly. The Pupation Phase moves the believer from chaos to cosmos through spiritual resurrection (from a sinful nature to a divine nature). This spiritual resurrection moves the believer away from fleshly driven desires to focus on things that are eternal in nature, no longer driven by lust. This is not to say that believers in the Pupation Phase want to experience fleshly desires. This spiritual resurrection is where the regenerated spirit of the believer emulates the physical attributes of the love of God (fruit of the Spirit and righteousness) through the obedience to the voice of the Holy Spirit.

Captivity Designed by God

If believers are going to experience God's glory (manifested goodness) they, too, must enter a place of restraints—a place where God can get the believer's undivided attention for protection and safekeeping until complete metamorphosis can be accomplished. The believer will need to commit to a place and time from their routine-daily activities to one sanctified to God. This commitment will ensure God's presence and provide a hiding place for peace, rest, serenity, and uninterrupted one-on-one time with the Holy Spirit for change.

In the book of Jeremiah, God caused his chosen people to be overtaken and held captive to receive a day of Sabbath, a day of rest, and a day of worship. This Sabbath rest is required for restoration which can only come from time spent with God. This Sabbath rest comes as believers sanctify a time and place of surrender to spiritual confinement, that the time in captivity will be considered holy unto God.

On several occasions, God prepared or caused his people (those who obeyed his commandment and feared him as their God) to be held in confinement to preserve or prepared them for his purpose. This captivity period is designed by God as the one who is the source of all power and authority. This captivity designed by God will provide safety and provisions for change as the believer obeys the commandments of God giving them an expected end. This is the kind of confinement that prompts believers to pray and praise God for his action to cause change in one's nature. Many times, this confinement may appear to be immobile, and nothing is happening, but the spirit of mankind is being renewed daily while camouflaged in a secret place designed by God.

The believer's zeal to commit to knowing (experiencing) God intimately will challenge what the believer assumed to be the *truth*. All that the believer has communicated while living in God's protected bubble (God's presence) without tangible proof will be challenged. The believer may understand that there has been a shift in their inner man (mankind's spirit) that cannot be explained at this phase of the metamorphosis.

This designed captivity for believers will challenge the believer's Soteriology (salvation). All that the believer has heard and repeated in conversation and prayer will have its adjudication process or the conclusion of the matter. While in the custody of the will of God for their lives, believers will find themselves unable to outsource help for life struggles of this dark world to gain victory or deliverance. Believers may experience isolation from people who once came to their rescue or aid in time past, now unavailable.

This captivity designed by God will move the believer from believing in the word of God to having faith in the gospel of Jesus Christ. This is where the believer moves from receiving Jesus as their personal Savior to Jesus as Lord and Savior. The believer's passion to follow Jesus Christ will require hearing the voice of the Holy Spirit and following the guidance provided without any reservation (doubt, skepticism).

This captivity is a place of no return (old nature). The journey will change the believer's thought process, concept of life, and see themselves as they are in God's sight. This is a place where the believer's resources are useless. God becomes the only source for daily survival, the only source as the old fleshly desires are tempted, the only source available in the midnight hours of despair, and the only source capable of restoration or deliverance.

Dying to Self

While in the cocoon the **caterpillar** digests **itself**, releasing enzymes to dissolve all its tissues. The caterpillar will fall apart and literally die to a nature that identifies it as a caterpillar.

The caterpillar digests itself and uses many of the cells of the formal part to build new parts for a new nature. The caterpillar will no longer crawl and hide underneath a leaf but grow wings and antennae for navigation in space and time. These formal parts have always been embedded in the caterpillar as the seed of the butterfly can only produce itself. These formal parts are restored as the caterpillar begins its transformation from a caterpillar to a butterfly. These formal parts begin to form and reestablish their purpose to glorify God.

Salvation is provided through the death and resurrection of Jesus Christ. Caterpillars have no reproduction ability by design and the existence of the butterfly depends on the death (separation) of the caterpillar and the reforming through the complete metamorphosis process. This death is significant as the caterpillar goes through their histogenesis transformation to a new nature—a nature designed by God for his glory.

Likewise, the believer's death (separation from self) will challenge their faith to present themselves as broken vessels. This death (separation) will challenge the believer's flesh to yield themselves to God (the potter) to be molded into true worshippers (circumcised in their spirit), worshipping God in spirit and in truth. This death (separation) is where believers count every crown, worldly credential, and worldly success as lost to know Christ and be found in him, not having one's own righteousness.

Furthermore, the prerequisite to follow Christ is to deny one's self and to die to self by surrendering to the will of God, putting aside selfish interests. The ability and empowerment to fully surrender to the will of God are not going to happen overnight. This summons (decree) is a lifelong event, fighting the good fight of faith while getting to know the Holy Spirit and his purpose in the believer's life. A believer's desire to endure the discomfort and daily disappointment in the flesh will cause great frustration. There will be more times than one can count of the many failures and disappointments in the believer's walk with God, the many shameful acts that do not represent the title(s) believers are identified by mankind in the church, and the many judgmental acts of self-righteousness toward others.

Similarly, believers have come to a crossroads where the image of the man in the mirror is reflecting themselves versus reflecting Christ, and do not align themselves to spiritual maturity/change. Dying to self is a prerequisite to following Jesus Christ. Dying to self allows the believer to begin the process of sanctification as it pertains to the acts of sin. This is the period God appears to be particularly close and hands-on in the life of the believer. God appears to be hands-on as it pertains to separating one's self from ungodly places of temptations and avoiding vain arguments. This challenge in the flesh will cause physical suffering and discomfort, as God reforms the believer. God must increase in the believer's life to become preeminent for change.

Dying to self is a place to love your neighbor and do whatever possible to edify them, whether they have a covenant with God or not. Dying to self is a place where believers do away with indecisive decisions—no more sudden changes or double-mindedness in their thinking. *The believer understands it's not through a moment of happiness or victories that the gift of the Holy Spirit is recognized, but a moment of attrition gradually reducing their own strength.* This call to die to self goes beyond the physicality and moves the believer to understand their created purpose, which is to worship God.

After thirty-plus years of praying and worshipping God, I'm still putting off the "old man" habits and putting on the newness of who and what God has prepared for me. The gospel of Jesus Christ is clear and the protocol to represent him in this world is tight and right. I continue to fall short time and time again, asking, begging, and pleading with God to provide another opportunity to get it right. This flesh of mine cannot be trusted, and the enemy uses every opportunity to lure believers away from the truth and provide options for what success looks like. We as believers don't have to work alone to accomplish deliverance, God's grace is more than enough to enable our success.

Breaking Up Fallow Ground

It is not enough to have witnessed Christ as Lord

and Savior while enduring many years of pain, suffering, failure, disappointments, broken relationships, etc. God knows who you are and has prepared a place beside him to produce the kind of fruit that will truly represent him, in and out of season. This place beside God (in agreement) is where believers separate themselves from hypocrisy, lifting up a standard that represents the God they serve. These believers seek to serve God in integrity at the level of God's faithfulness toward his word.

Here lies an opportunity to break up the fallow ground in one's life for preparation to present themselves as living sacrifices of God's power and presence in this world. This is the season believers break up the old habits that rendered no fruit for unbelievers and break up the pain of past failed relationships that caused havoc in the lives of all associated. This is the season for breaking up fallow ground that will allow believers to disconnect themselves from worldliness and its systems. This is the place believers denounce worldly success based on worldly standards.

Breaking up the fallow ground in one's life will allow the incorruptible seed space and time to produce the fruit of the Holy Spirit—one of unselfish concern for others, displaying an enter peace that can be seen by mankind, being consistence in the storm—kindness, goodness, self-control to mention a few.

This phase of putting off the old nature and breaking up the fallow ground in the believer's life is vital to the expansion of the Kingdom of God. If the lost have no witness, have no example(s) of God's grace, where do they get the truth? This breaking of fallow ground will allow believers to act as midwives to those waiting on the sons and daughters of God to show forth God's presence. Breaking up one's fallow ground will give room for the Holy Spirit's gifts to operate in the believer's life. These gifts of the Holy Spirit enable the believers to become midwives with a motive of the love of God.

God's love will produce midwives that are not seeking identification for praise, nor seeking rewards or compensations for the work(s) of the Holy Spirit.

God's love as a motive will shine a light in a dark place to help their neighbor in a time of need. God's love as a motive will produce the kind of midwives that guide and assist in difficult times and physical, emotional, and spiritual transitions. Believers under the authority of God's love will provide power to endure the storms of the enemy. Believers under God's love/anointing will exercise the gift of discernment seeing what the birth-giver can't see, recognizing the signs of transition, and witnessing the crowning of newness in other's lives and victory over defeat.

It's God's grace and the believer's commitment to

surrender to the voice of the Holy Spirit that cleansing and purging of the soul is accomplished. This is where the desire to be more like Christ beckons the believer to put away anything that negatively influences their decision-making process. The believer puts away anything that might energize the fleshly desires and appetite of worldly fashions. This effort to break up one's fallow ground is to present oneself as a vessel of honor sanctified to God. This is the place where spiritual purging is not putting new over the old, but starting anew with an empty vessel in the fear of God.

The believer's commitment to break up their fallow ground will provide spiritual blessings as God causes all things to work out for their good. Their previous acts of sin no longer allow past experiences to prevent them from sowing righteousness in their lives. Believers no longer allow past experiences of hurt, bitterness, unforgiveness, rejection, and selfishness to hinder the work of the indwelling Holy Spirit. This breaking up fallow ground requires God's power for molding, establishing, and appointing the believer to a position of change. This is the place believers begin to display the commandment of God to add virtue to their newly found unwavering faith, no longer excited about the fruit of this world and tales of its false representations of the blessings of God (boasting regarding the haves and the have-nots). A place where believers are aimed to have their moral character influenced by the word of God and the unction (anointing) of the Holy Spirit.

Renewed Nature

The caterpillar's body is liquefied and histogenesis (God's created concept) takes place, using predestined attributes to reconstruct the caterpillar to a renewed nature (butterfly). This is the Pupation Phase of the metamorphosis where the caterpillar, while in the cocoon (captivity), puts on the new nature.

Likewise, the believer is called to be transformed (metamorphosis) from a sinful nature to a divine nature. The gifts and talents of God are without repentance embedded in the heart of mankind before the foundation of the world. Liken unto the caterpillar, the spiritual attributes (image and likeness of God) for mankind's divine nature are embedded in their hearts before the foundation of the world that believers should be holy and without blame before God. The spiritual renewing at the Sheep Gate awakens God's spiritual plans predesigned before the foundation of the world. God's plan for mankind's life was interrupted through physical birth inheriting the sinful nature of a physical father.

The process inside the cocoon is vigorous and powerful as the caterpillar's body basically is liquefied by digestive fluids and the body is restructured using specialized formative cells. This process is called histogenesis, in which undifferentiated (specific cells not yet changed) cells are used to build different body tissues.

Liken unto the caterpillar, the enzymes released to dissolve mankind's "spiritual tissue" for forming and reestablishing its purpose are the ingredients of the bread of life for spiritual digestion and reforming. This enzyme (bread of life) is the substance produced by the living word of God, which acts as a catalyst to bring about a specific spiritual reaction and change.

Similarly, believers pass through a spiritual histogenesis (an idealized mental image of Christ) where the seed of the bread of life is the only influence. The believer's old nature is passed away and all things become new as the food source (bread of life) reproduces itself. The old stony heart of the believer's formal nature is being used to develop a heart of love for mankind. This is the place where spiritual histogenesis takes place by which God works out all things for the believer's good (synergism). The believer's faith and confidence are expressed while evangelizing in the Fish Gate, and the personal experience in the Valley Gate differentiates (transforms, converts) the old man's spiritual nature to a nature liken unto Christ. The believer is no longer hiding in the rear of the church among the congregation to avoid conversations regarding their faith. The believer is no longer fearful of their faith as their regenerated spirit has equipped them to receive spiritual things.

The believer's spirit goes through a digestion process as the designated food source (bread of life) begins to reproduce itself, renewing the believer's spirit to the image of Christ. This digestion of the believer's spirit changes the purpose of the inner parts (spirit) of the believer to take on the image of Christ, reuniting and repairing the gap between mankind and God.

This digestion process prompts the believer to consider denying themselves of the temptation of the things of this world and begin to focus on things that are eternal. *This spiritual digestion process is where the believer becomes strong in their convictions of faith, no longer depending on personal resources and worldly ambitions for self-identification.* This is the place believers acknowledge the power of God in their lives "that it's not I, but God who works in me and through me to do his good will." The believer understands nothing can be accomplished without Christ and there is no good thing in mankind's flesh and mankind will never be fleshless in this world. There is an old saying, "Born once—die twice; born twice—die once."

Spiritual Growth

The Pupation Phase of the spiritual metamorphosis consists of the Valley, Dung, and Fountain Gates.

The Valley Gate (Baptism by Fire)

The spiritual growth for the believer moves from the sheep gate (salvation), through the Fish Gate (servicehood), the Old Gate (foundational truth), and into the Valley Gate, where a relationship with God develops humility through the works of the Holy Spirit. The spiritual growth for the believer continues as the believer yields to the voice of the Holy Spirit, spreading their wings beyond the outer court of the tabernacle (believing only what can be seen), seeking the Kingdom of God.

The Valley Gate is the beginning of the complete metamorphosis to change one's sinful nature to a nature designed by God. This Pupation Phase of the metamorphosis is where the believer commits to making Jesus not only their Savior but also Lord over their life. It's not enough to have feasted on the designated food source and believe—nor strongly voiced the word of God while in the Fish Gate—it's time to witness the will of God for themselves and begin trusting and relying on his promises.

Like the butterfly, the end state of mankind is designed to glorify God and commune (sharing one's heart and mind in prayer) with him. Getting to know God is a lifetime experience as mankind knows in part, receives in part, and understands in part. We as believers must keep in mind that eternal life is tied to knowing God, the only true God, and Jesus Christ whom he sent. The lack of this knowledge will rob mankind of peace, rest, and joy. Without this knowledge, the believer's faith is limited, as it pertains to the spiritual power of God and their capacity to have life on earth and eternal life with God.

I recall my prior Valley Gate experience, having no wisdom, no understanding of who God was in my life. The Sheep Gate experience had brought me to a place I could voice my understanding in conversation without the fear of ignorance I once dreaded. The conversation had no spiritual growth as the circle (church folk) I surrounded myself in repeated the same biblical stories. The same understanding of the scripture preached at the church with no wisdom (spiritual insight) or understanding. The fellowship after church meetings was exciting and I was part of the "fraternity" (brotherhood).

However, the more time I spent with God in prayer and reading his word, the more I understood there was much more than what the preacher expressed on Sunday. If the word of God wasn't causing change in my ungodly habits, character, attitude, behavior, or lifestyle, then what have I achieved? I recognized it was time to not only enroll in the Valley Gate experience but complete the Valley Gate by putting the Sheep and Fish Gate victories behind me. The scripture that prompted my decision to complete the Valley Gate states, "How will we escape [the penalty] if we ignore so great a salvation?" Being saved and behaving in an ungodly spirit didn't agree with my regenerated spirit and rest was hard to come by.

Believers are asked to commit to the Valley Gate to further their faith in the gospel of Jesus Christ. This commitment is an effort to demonstrate that what can be seen above the iceberg of the believer (behavior, language, actions, nature of the caterpillar) reflects the organic being beneath the iceberg (grace of God, love of God, mercy of God, useful qualities, gifts of the Spirit).

The Valley Gate is where self-investigation takes place and the image of what is reflected in the mirror versus what is reflected through the lens of God requires many changes. The driving force behind the believer enrolling in the Valley Gate is the indwelling Holy Spirit, as the believer begins to crave and desire being more like Christ and living a life of holiness—holiness where sanctification, consecration, and dedication to God are practiced and exercised. The kind of holiness where the believer separates themselves from the world and worldliness.

The Valley Gate is a place where the believer becomes faithful in the spiritual weight room (exercising what is believed), honoring God by trusting him with or without noticeable evidence of change. The results of the Valley Gate will provide proof (tangible and intangible) of God's power unspeakable, God's knowledge unsearchable, and God's presence unimaginable. The Valley Gate is a time and place sanctified by the believer, moving them from a place of comfort and into a place of true faith—a time and place to exercise the believer's spiritual muscle associated with feasting on the designed food source digested in the Larva Phase.

The Valley Gate is where believers will receive and understand God's grace (love) and develop humility. This is the place the believer becomes naked and no longer ashamed before God in prayer, praise, and worship. The believer is no longer praying the prayer, "If I've done anything wrong, please forgive me," to a more honest and direct prayer of faith (knowledge of the believer's error) with humility and honesty (integrity) before God. The Valley Gate is the place where believers recognize the thorn(s) and shortcomings in one's life and build faith to overcome them through the work of the Holy Spirit. This is the place where the believer will get to know the Holy Spirit in his full capacity as a comforter, helper, advocate, intercessor, and the believer's voice of faith. The Valley Gate is a place where the believer comes to the end of themselves so that they might empty themselves in the presence of the sound of many waters before God in prayer. A place where believers wrestle no longer with the things of this world, and thorns in their lives allow grace to be perfected through little strength within themselves.

As the believer enters the Brook of Jabbok (place to empty one's self), they receive the ministry of reconciliation and understand that by walking in agreement with Christ they can:

- overcome their fears;
- overcome their shortcomings;
- overcome their weaknesses and commit to change.

The believer's relationship with God will need to be authentic in every sense of the word. The Brook of Jabbok is where the believer will empty themselves of everything that identifies them (worldly credentials, crowns of success, gifts, talents) as a gentile in this world (having no covenant with God).

The Valley Gate is where the believer will experience God's power and constant presence in their lives. This is the place where tangible and intangible evidence of Christ's resurrection will be unveiled to the believer as they seek the Kingdom of God. This revealing will provide full assurance that the believer:

- is justified (righteous in God's sight)

before God because of the work of Jesus Christ on the cross;
- has been provided access to God;
- no longer fears the sting of death;
- has union with Christ made possible by his resurrection thereby receiving their righteousness accepted by God.

This is the place where the believer will gain valuable revelation and knowledge that their will is inadequate to obey God's word and their little faith (strength) is the favor of God. Much lip service regarding the believer's faith in the word of God has taken place to this point without tangible or intangible proof that God's word is true.

This is the time and place the believer brags and boasts regarding their Soteria (deliverance) without personally experiencing the cost that led to their steadfastness, patience, and confidence to receive deliverance by the Kingdom of God (God's constitutional rights for believers). This is the place spiritual challenge(s) and practical testing of the believer's faith will be on center stage.

The Valley Gate Experience

As we previously discussed in the believer's Sheep Gate experience, we were met with unknown and unseen forces that defile logic and mankind's intellect to express to others this change in nature.

The believer's Fish Gate experience was filled with words of exaltation and power without tangible evidence and revelation knowledge to fully express in words. The Valley Gate experience will provide undisputed evidence that God's word is true, and Jesus Christ is the son of the living God. The Valley Gate experience is designed to build the believer up and cause them to develop the kind of faith whereby the believer is fully persuaded in their own mind that Jesus is Lord.

Before taking care of God's sheep, testing and spiritual development in the Valley Gate (in the spiritual weight room) are essential to followers of Jesus Christ.

A relationship with the trinity (God, Jesus, and the Holy Spirit) transcends the believer from a relationship with God to a covenant. This covenant requires more than a confession of sin, more than digesting the designed food source (the word of God), more than words of exaltation, more than a conversation about God. It requires a conversation about who God is and the believer's purpose to be transformed. This covenant relationship presents the believer as a living sacrifice, true ambassador of Christ, true witness of the gospel of Jesus Christ, and the Amen of God's word.

The Valley Gate experience is where the word of God is manifested through fire (trails), developing and establishing godly behaviors. It's through the trying of the believer's faith that patience (steadfastness in the word of God) is developed, having no need for the things of this world nor an appetite for the world's fashion. This is the gate where the believer establishes an intimate relationship with God to come boldly to the throne room of grace with clean hands and a pure heart, asking God for his ways and for his wisdom. It's in this fire (trial) that the believer begins to understand God foreknew the time of their appointment (existence) and the bond of their habitation and that it's God's will (permissive) being executed in their lives in his presence.

This is the gate where the believer establishes their own precepts and concepts based on the Rhema word of God (revelation knowledge/application) while in the Valley Gate. Believers understand their bodies are the temple of the Holy Spirit, which is of God, and the believer is to use their bodies as living sacrifices for God's goodness and purpose. This is the gate where the believer recognizes that their every move and very being is being directed by the Holy Spirit, allowing Christ to live through them. The results of the Valley Gate find the believer, edified in the gospel of the grace of God, able to testify this grace through the ministry of reconciliation. Believers receive the gift of God (gospel of God's grace) that takes on the form of divine favor, sharing in the divine life of God.

The believer's experience in the Valley Gate will gain revelation knowledge and humility designed for their spiritual conversion that can only be filled through the baptism of the Holy Spirit with fire.

The Valley Gate experience will develop the kind of faith that staggers not at the promises of the word of God. Believers will experience God is faithful to what he said he would do, and he is not slack concerning his promises. The Valley Gate experience transcends the believer's narrative from prayer to divine certainty.

This Valley Gate experience will propel the believer to a place of yes and Amen to the promises of God's word. A place where patience and humility are perfected. A place where patience (steadfast during trials) is allowed to have perfect work through the trying of the believer's faith. A place where the believer is calling on God to bring them out of the bondage of their mind and liberate their soul as evidence of his presence in the believer's life.

The Valley Gate will reveal the person of God. This revelation will amplify the believer's access to God while experiencing the essence of his being. The person of God will share an infinite God to a finite man through faith, while trusting and relying on God's word.

The Pupation Phase (Valley Gate) is where the

"rubber meets the road." It's time to cut the umbilical cord from the world and its systems. It's time to get out from among the heavily dependent and close relationship with the world's fashion and ideas. It's time to consider the eternal forecast rather than next week's events, to consider becoming a conduit through which the power of God is transferred through the believer to cause a change in another's life. The Valley Gate is a place where believers will experience the power of God, the power of Jesus's resurrection, the works and functions of the indwelling Holy Spirit, and receive Jesus Christ not as their Savior only, but now as their Lord.

When a believer receives Jesus as their personal Savior, they also receive Jesus in his glory to include his Lordship (yielding/total unreserved obedience) over their lives. From the Sheep Gate until now, believers only understand and react to Jesus as their Savior. Believers experiencing the person of God for their lives will provide confidence and unshakeable faith in the power of God and his might.

For Jesus to become their Lord, tangible and intangible proofs are required to gain the believer's confidence in the word of God. It's through this confidence the believer clearly hears and understands the voice of God through the Holy Spirit. Jesus, as Lord, requires yielding to his authority and lordship to obey God's word and understanding the love of God is unconditional.

The Valley Gate experience is designed to cause the believer to lean on God's word with absolute trust and confidence in his power, not the believer's earthly resources. From my perspective, this is the spiritual gate many believers enter and find themselves unconsciously comfortable with the victory(s) of the Sheep, Fish, and Old Gates.

I recall my personal Valley Gate experience having been removed from the spiritual teaching of the gospel that once kept me grounded to a place where I was left to defend on my own. A place with physical resources but no spiritual nutrients to continue my growth in Christ. The spiritual battles in my mind began, and I was not properly trained to handle them.

I've asked myself many times, "Am I saved?" It sure didn't *feel* like it, and my struggle only got worse as I impatiently waited on God to come and rescue me. I began reading scriptures that pertained to my circumstances following the pattern of others based on their stories (inspiration books), seeking anyone that could explain to me what I was doing wrong. How could this be? Saved but defeated. Spiritually having access to the source of all power, seated with Christ in heavenly places and yet struggling with the battle of the mind. Full of the gospel of Jesus Christ, expressed in every walk of life, standing tall, and looking good before the church, expressing my conviction with words of joy, honoring God with my lips with no tangible evidence that his word is true. Yes, there were intangible proofs that could not be explained at that point of my metamorphosis.

The struggle only continued in other areas of my life as I cried out to God day and night. I had voiced God's word with great trust to all I had encountered and now, while isolated without a lifeline from spiritual gatekeepers, I was lost and disoriented, unable to navigate my spiritual compass. I recall asking God in prayer, "Where are you? I need you and your word said you would help me in time of trouble, that you know all things." My prayer was, "Help me with my struggle as I wrestle with my salvation (deliverance)." The enemy would challenge me at every turn, he would do anything to ensure that the word of God didn't come to pass in my life. Because of the lack of experience with God's power, doubt and trouble found its way into my life. A narrative of unbelief permeated with consistency and unconsciously dictated what would show up in my life. The lack of financial resources to maintain the family at a level of comfort once enjoyed was troubled, miniature arguments with my spouse led to sleepless nights, relationships with family members who once relied on me for worldly resources were now suffering, persecution from friends and work-related issues through the stress of it all, I now pondered. "Who am I?" I asked.

The Valley Gate is the place where the rubber

meets the road. I refuse to turn back to the world that offered me nothing and the old ways of solving my issues through borrowing and pleading with others to come to my aid in fear. Later, I came to recognize it wasn't so much fear as it was pride that caused me to fight. The fighting spirit, stubbornness, and pride inherited from my forefathers took over. The word of God poured out of my mouth, honoring God with my lips, but my heart was distant, not ready to totally trust and rely on God's word. I hadn't experienced a level in God where confidence and patience joined forces, empowering me to receive the promises of God. I couldn't go back on the words that already preceded out of my mouth, and pride deprived me of asking for help from those who God had sent to my aid. I was too prideful to ask the pastor and the church for prayer, too prideful to let go and let God because, it appeared, he was taking his time.

Real prayer doesn't express itself until one is desperate. Although the Holy Spirit was shouting out guidance, the many sounds of doubt and worldly chatter muzzled his voice, and I didn't have the inclination to stop and listen. God will show up in his own way and his timing is not necessarily how we expect. I recall a telephone call, at my workplace, of some disturbing news. As I was driving home to handle the situation, I cried out to God, "What's next? Why won't you help me?" My spirit got quiet enough to hear the Holy Spirit say, "Look at the man on the side of the road walking toward you." I ignored the voice I knew was the Holy Spirit, as the man on the side of the road couldn't help me. For most of my prayers, I had asked the Holy Spirit to be a loud voice within me—even hit me in the head if needed to get my attention. I finally looked at the man on the side of the road and he wore a T-shirt that read, "I Have Everything Under Control." My narrative changed and faith showed up with great conviction.

Getting quiet before God, listening, and obeying the voice of the Holy Spirit would be the vehicle that would cause triumph in my life. The Holy Spirit brought back remembrances of God's word and I found rest in the scripture, "I'll never leave you nor forsake you." God said he knows how much I could bear and will make a way of escape/deliverance in his timing for my spiritual growth. God knows that going through trouble/trials will better a relationship with him as I call on him to deliver me. I would seek refuge in him. The more believers receive from God, the less they will need of mankind.

It is this struggle through God's protection and camouflage that allowed me to endure, resulting in experiencing the person of God (Jehovah-jireh, Nissi, Rapha, Rophe, Makadesh, Shammah, etc.). As I look back, God was working his will in me while changing my spiritual nature and narrative.

The Valley Gate experience is the place ambassadors for Christ are born, a place where the believer is clothed in humility, and where truth and faith are the believer's default. God wants every believer to run the race set before them in confidence (fearless faith) that God is with them, and nothing can stop them.

"No fire can burn them; no battle can turn them; no mountain can stop them, and no giant can defeat them." —Tasha Cobb

Application

Who is Christ to you? What have you experienced time and time again where the gospel of Jesus Christ has delivered you? Where have the unexplainable victories puzzled you through fervent prayer, praise, and worship? A time when you boast to others regarding the peace you have during a storm, the battle(s) won in the courtroom without representation of the system, the ability to maintain a level of life without worldly resources. Is the darkness of this world challenging your faith?

The Dung Gate (Deny Self)

The believer's spiritual growth continues from the Valley Gate that produced humility and experiencing the person of God has prepared the believer to see themselves before a Holy God.

The Dung Gate is where garbage, ruin, and waste material are taken away. This gate leads to the spiritual health and wealth of the believer's mind, soul, and body. This is the place where the habits of the formal sinful nature and its pleasures are no longer desired. A successful Valley Gate experience will provide insight into the merging with Christ, identified by godly sorrow and repentance. The Gung Gate experience is of great significance to the believer. The Dung Gate is a threshold, connecting godly behaviors with the fruit of the Spirit of God.

The Dung Gate is a place where believers recognize that God's grace is sufficient for any challenges they might encounter. This is the place where believers recognize that the person of God found in the Valley Gate is more than able and willing to rid them of their old nature. This is the place where believers cry out to God in their weaknesses while boasting in their infirmities to ensure the power of Christ rest upon them. This is a place of renewed purpose and attributes to fulfill what's at the heart of mankind—to worship a Holy God. The Dung Gate is where believers understand entering the presence of God requires clean hands and a pure heart and surrender into his hands for forming. This is the gate believers seek to become true worshippers, who worship God in spirit and truth, fulfilling God's will for mankind.

The believer is saved by grace but defeated in their nature as the old man continues to have influence on the flesh and its behavior. The many years of perfecting the fleshly desires and enjoying the acts of sin and the many habits that shaped the believer's character are not easily put away. The believer's spirit has passed from death (a spirit separated from God) to life (a regenerated spirit alive to God). The born-again spirit has no pleasure in the joy the sinful flesh once desired. The man in the mirror is no longer pleasing in God's sight—the man in the mirror is ashamed and embarrassed regarding their thoughts and behavior toward others. The believer's godly sorrow (repentance) based on the word of God and faith expressed in the Fish Gate is out of calibration. The believer's moral compass has been taken over by the cares, fashion, and change in culture of this world and its systems.

God knows the believer's deeds and their neophyte level of understanding and has set before them an open door to move from the cross (suffering Savior) to perfection (sovereign Savior). The believer's little strength in self is a positive attribute and will be honored by God. Because of the little strength at this junction of the believer's life, much faith and trust in God's ability will be sought after while denying self.

The word of God instructs believers to put away any sort of idolatry (loving anything more than God), and anything that will replace one's devotion to God. The followers of Christ will be challenged regarding the cost to follow Christ, the cost to be molded into the image of Christ, the cost of the separation of their fleshly desires, the cost of humility, patience, meekness, and the fruit of the Holy Spirit.

This is the place where the believer recognizes the reverential fear of God expressed through entering his gates in prayer with a pure heart (one who has empathy for others, makes others feel cared for, a giver and welcoming), and clean hands (one who understands they are blameless and innocent before God because of the work of Christ on the cross and their faith). The believer's zeal to know God and experience Jesus's resurrection power (new creation, more than a conqueror) will be challenged in the Dung Gate. Like the prerequisite to enter the metamorphosis process, one must be born again. The believer unknowingly has already experienced the resurrection power of Christ (salvation). Now they seek to understand the life (in Christ Jesus) after death (separated from God). This is where the believer shuts down, surrenders to the voice of the Holy Spirit, and removes the "bit" that controls their thought process.

This is the place where believers move beyond the

power of the gospel of Christ to perfection which requires working out one's own salvation through fear and trembling. The believer's will and made-up mind are not enough to overcome this dark world and the wiles of the enemy. The badge of salvation is not enough to endure the good fight of faith nor to demonstrate change in one's ability to put off the old nature's habits.

David, a man after God's own heart, acknowledged his fleshly deficiencies, lack of authority, and power to change them. David, in prayer, asked God to blot out his transgressions, wash him from his iniquities, and cleanse him from the sinful nature molded at birth. By the same token, believers are aware of their transgressions and the fleshly acts of sin embedded in their members from physical birth. Believers will experience the same struggles to put away childish things and grow up in the teaching of wisdom from the word of God.

The Dung Gate is the place believers begin to reminisce and acknowledge the gifts and talents of God in their lives and cultivate their fallow ground to free themselves from themselves. The Dung Gate is the place where the believer prepares themselves for the holiness and righteousness of God to overtake them and bring every evil work, sinful habit, and condemnation into captivity.

It's time to accept the Dung Gate with confidence

and humility that God is ready and able to change the reflection and the nature of the reflection in the mirror. This call to holiness is a commandment of God and will further the metamorphosis, putting off the old nature and putting on the new divine nature. True evidence of regeneration in the believer's life will display the image of God's character and nature as a witness of God's love for mankind.

The Dung Gate Experience

After successfully fighting the good fight of faith in the Valley Gate, the believer has positioned themselves to begin the lifelong task of ridding themselves of anything that is not pleasing in God's sight. Through much prayer and supplication and the works of the Holy Spirit, change is imminent for edification for the body of Christ. It is at this point of the believer's journey that the believer understands God's commandment to be transformed is bigger than their ambitions and bigger than their crowns of victories and the accolades received by man only to be cast at Jesus's feet.

The believer's fleshly habits are yet alive and hindering the fruit(s) of the promises of God. This is the junction where the believer not only recognizes whatever defiles them but moves from the outer courts of the tabernacle into the presence of God with clean hands and a pure heart. Through the gifts of the Holy Spirit and the believer's willingness to hear and adhere to the Holy Spirit's voice, believers begin putting off the old man and begin putting on the new man.

This phase of the metamorphosis is literally moving the believer from a place to empty one's self (Brook Jabbok) to a place of newness of life (Joppa). This is a true representation of service to God. The believer's faith in the person of God has provided them a lifeline for change.

This move of faith, confidence, and humility acts as a law to adjust the perception of the physical man in the mirror with confidence through the fear of God that all things are possible in him. The believer becomes aware of their shortcomings, viewing themselves through the lens of God's word.

The believer clearly sees their thongs in the flesh and the depravity that once separated them from God. The Dung Gate experience is where sanctification and love are demonstrated in the believer's walk with an attitude expressing their gratitude for God's love, grace, and salvation (mercy). An attitude to pursue the things that are above, things that are eternal, things that are pleasing in God's sight, fulfilling the will of God. Believers are challenged to take on the task to walk circumspectly as ambassadors and agents of God, always ready and available to the ministry of reconciliation. This is the place where believers witness the power of the gospel to tell the story to mankind to lay aside their war against God, lay aside their ignorance of who God is, and be reconciled to God. We as believers become specimens and living proof that mankind can live in harmony with God as sons and daughters of God. Through the grace of God, mankind can return to their origin of existence, consistent with having been made in the likeness and image of God.

"O wretched man that I am! who shall deliver me from the body of this death [this sinful nature]?" The sooner believers acknowledge that the old sinful nature cannot be defeated and put away within their own strength and resources, the sooner the gifts of the Holy Spirit and the grace of God are sought after for deliverance. The power to say no to sin nor the believer's will is sufficient to prevail over the sinful nature and habits that have perfected themselves over many years with an unregenerated spirit.

This is the gate where believers understand the sin of the old nature is yet alive in their members, inherited through physical birth, and the challenge in the flesh to become true ambassadors of Christ will require much time to accomplish.

God wants to form the believer, reestablish, and change their very nature to the likeness and nature of Christ.

Crucified with Christ: The Dung Gate Experience

It's the crucified believers who are at peace with God through faith in Jesus Christ. Believers received this crucifixion by faith, understanding they have been crucified in the flesh—their flesh has been nailed to a cross, no longer bound by its desires and appetites. The designed food source (bread of life) for believers is received and believed without hesitation having endured the Valley Gate experience. The old man has died and the life he once expressed is being renewed daily from the seed results of the designed food source.

The task at hand to put off the old man in the Dung Gate is faced with merging the new man being developed daily. Believers cannot continue to practice sin by yielding their members as vessels of unrighteous acts and a false representation of Christ which opposes the badge of salvation. A believer's confession and profession of faith are in a God who delivers. Having experienced a regenerated spirit—having the ability to commune with God through the power of the Holy Spirit—believers must love God fervently with all their heart, soul, and mind so that they might serve God with the newness of life. Believers must make a conscious decision to put on the new man as living sacrifices for God, set apart for his plan and purpose for their lives. This is the time and place believers consecrate themselves (body, soul, and mind), answering the effectual calling of God (devoted to the worship of God).

This is the intent and objective of the commandment of God, that believers must be transformed (metamorphosis) to rid themselves of the old nature, equipping them with the ability to walk in the newness of life. The believer's designed food source is going to be the final answer to putting on the new man while putting off the old man's nature (habits). The word of God (seed) will establish a standard for believers to conduct themselves as they renew their minds with the bread of life. It's through this renewing that believers will trust and rely on the power of God's might to assist with putting off the old man and putting on the new.

Crucified believers that understand they are no longer alienated from God are now saints of the Kingdom of God and the glorious gospel of Christ. Crucified believers no longer confused about who they are in Christ do not have their eyes blinded and their hearts hardened, unable to see the unseen. Crucified believers understand they are perfect and wonderfully made and loved by God. Crucified believers put away the works of unclean acts and the old man's selfish desires of things of this world. The believer's zeal to approach a Holy God is desired and sought after with great diligence.

Crucified believers consider the words of their professions and the root of their existence. The tongue of the believer will require serious revamping. The words of the believer's mouth are vital to putting off the old man and putting on the new man. The word of God declares that the tongue is yet a small member of the body but sets fire to, or contaminates, the entire body.

Ironically, while believers are putting on the new man, grace and truth are going to be their watchwords. This new man's nature will move the believer to a level of maturity in the Dung Gate where love is their default action and reaction in their daily walk with Christ. This is a mature level in Christ, where discernment of the spirit profited much, and the believer is sober, vigilant, and walking circumspectly in the gifts of the Holy Spirit. One of the gifts of the Holy Spirit is love. Love is the source of grace. When love is expressed, grace has space and time to intervene, to act as an enabler to cause change.

The old nature of the believer is yet alive, battling for supremacy to control the believer's thoughts, mind, and conscience and the very essence of the believer's decision-making process. The motions of sins continue to work in the believer's members to bring forth the wages of sin, hindering the believer to serve their God in the newness of their spirit. The battle of the mind began, and the will of man is challenged daily, but the believer's spirit is renewed day by day while feasting on the bread of life.

Many years ago, while in the Dung Gate, I asked myself, *Where do I start to rid these influences and fleshly desires that kept me hostage when I desire to do good?* I remember jotting down the fruits of the flesh from the scriptures. Then decided which one I had challenges with so that I might create an order-of-merit list to deal with them one by one. Several years passed, and I was still working on the first fruit selected, as the flesh is sinful and prayer and my will to do good didn't always prevail. The order-of-merit list was useless, and the fruit of the flesh deceived me. "O wretched man that I am! who shall deliver me from this body of death?"

I thank my God through Jesus Christ, that in his presence is liberty. Jesus is Lord over my life, and it is he that will provide the strength, knowledge, and wisdom to overcome my infirmities.

If the believer will yield to the voice of the three witnesses (Holy Spirit, water, and the blood) present on this earth, the fight of faith becomes light, and rest from one's work to overcome the thongs in their lives is inevitable.

Application

Are you aware there is a need for daily cleansing from sinful acts and fleshly habits? Are you aware that the wages of unrepented sinful acts affect a believer's communion with God, prayer to God, and fellowship with others?

God has made a way of escape by asking for forgiveness with a pure heart and godly sorrow. Ask God to help you with daily cleansing through the knowledge, understanding, wisdom, and counsel of his word.

The Dung Gate is having a naked and unashamed experience getting rid of whatsoever not of God, casting down imaginations and every high thing that exalts itself against the knowledge of God, and bringing into captivity every thought to the obedience of Christ. Cleansing is available through the word and power of the word of God. Cleansing is available through confessing our sins, as God is faithful and just to forgive the believer of their sins and cleanse them from all unrighteousness.

The Fountain Gate (Filled Spirit)

The Fountain Gate is a picture of the Holy Spirit not to be confused with the presence indwelling Spirit of God. This is the filling of the Holy Spirit for God's purposes only. The Fountain Gate is the place where the light of the word of God is evangelized, resulting in living water from the changed nature of the believer through a successful Valley Gate where humility and holiness are established.

The Fountain Gate is the place where power from an outside source will assist the believer in their covenant with God to fulfill the ministry of reconciliation. The word of God declares the filling of the Holy Spirit is a gift from God. No one can purchase or earn this filling. God fills those who obey his commandment, those whom he can trust with the gospel, and those who have clean hands and a pure heart. It is in God's divine timing that he fills his people to carry out a task that cannot be accomplished in the flesh. This effort keeps the believer grounded and rooted in the need to be readily available for God's use. The believer understands they have no pressure to cause the word of God to come to pass. This is the gate believers will understand the little strength in themselves is greater than the expectations of others. Because God is the source provider of this filling, he gets all the praise, all the honor, all the glory, and all the worship.

Believers having successfully completed the Valley Gate have:

- witnessed the power of God's grace;
- gained confidence and patience in the face of provocation;
- obtained the attributes necessary to equip themselves with their predestined talents and spiritual gifts from God.

The Fountain Gate is where Jesus the person becomes a reality (omnipresent).

Through a successful Fountain Gate, the believer understands:

- the presence of Jesus is eternal and leads them beside the still waters;
- that Jesus redeemed them;
- Jesus called them by name.

This is the phase of the metamorphosis where rivers of living water are now touching and influencing their life and the lives of those God has put in their midst.

The Fountain Gate is where the gift of the Holy Spirit is on display for mankind to witness, a place where the believer unconsciously portrays the love of God toward mankind. The Fountain Gate is God's authority and power upon the believer to accomplish God's will to edify and expand the Kingdom of God. This is the gate where believers move from being mentally conscious to spiritually conscious.

The Fountain Gate Experience

The caterpillar has become a butterfly with all the necessary attributes to fulfill its purpose (to glorify God). The physical attributes are clearly seen. The butterfly's ability to win the struggle,

> *to force blood into its wings, to expand them for flight is required. This is a natural-birth phenomenal process and is necessary for strength building. If the butterfly, with all its new nature attributes, is unable to endure and complete this exercise, the butterfly will never fly and ultimately return to the nature of its former behavior as a caterpillar.*

Likewise, the believer will labor all the days of their lives, putting off the old nature and putting on the new nature in the spiritual realm. The believer has experienced and developed humility in the Valley Gate, cleansing and purification in the Dung Gate, and now requires the fullness of the Holy Spirit in the Fountain Gate for future commitment and endurance to complete the calling of God. Without the filling of the Holy Spirit, believers are limited to exercising the calling of God and his purpose for the believer's life. Without the filling of the Holy Spirit, a believer's ability to worship, serve, and obey a Holy God is undoable. Holiness (Qadash) requires sanctification (free from the penalty of sin), dedication (devotion to God's purpose), and consecration (believers answering God's spiritual calling). Feasting on the word of God and the believer's willpower cannot be trusted to carry out God's plan of restoration. This is the place where the heart of the believer is expressed through their sacrifice of praise.

This is the place and time the believer is honoring God with the fruit of their lips through the outpouring of the filling of the Holy Spirit.

This new Fountain Gate experience is where the gifts and talents of God are revealed and the provisions and providence for its desired outcome will depend on the living water at the Fountain Gate. This living water is Jesus Christ himself; the filling of the Holy Spirit is the gift of God to mankind. This is the gate where the gifts of the Holy Spirit will overtake the believer's spirit, causing an enlightened illumination within the soul of the believer. This filling of the Holy Spirit—refreshing water of life—cannot be purchased with a price, cannot be handed down as an inheritance.

This refreshing, illuminating outpour is a gift from God to whosoever is pleasing in his sight. The refreshing of the Holy Spirit (filling) provides a new strength never experienced before—able to stand until wisdom and understanding of the word of God is revealed. This refreshing, illuminating outpour of the Holy Spirit in the life of the believer transgresses logic. This living water (outpouring of the Holy Spirit) is where analytical research is unfounded and cannot be reasonably rationalized as God's riches are unsearchable.

This gift of living water will provide eternal life, safety, peace, joy, power, and all the fruit of the Spirit of God or God's presence in the life of the believer.

The Fountain Gate is where love, grace, and worship begin bubbling up in the heart of the believer. This is the phase of the metamorphosis where wells of living water are flowing outward from the believer to whosoever God has arranged to hear and see the salvation of Jesus the Christ.

This is the place where believers will make a conscious decision to make Jesus preeminent (foremost) in their lives. This is the gate where believers take no thought without consulting with Jesus, who sits at the head of the believer's faith. Jesus is the creator and originator who gave existence to the believer's faith. It is Jesus who scribed the truth of the word of God on the tables of the believer's heart, not with ink but by the Holy Spirit. It is Jesus who is the finisher of the believer's faith. This living water is Jesus, who is seated at the right hand of God in the place of authority, as the believer's advocate. Jesus is the one who puts an end to or completes the faith of the believer's words. Believers are God's workmanship unto good works to complete the metamorphosis for reproduction purposes to continue the will of God that none shall perish.

This is a place where the believer's outpours of gratitude for God's intervention and presence in the life of the believer are displayed daily. The Fountain Gate experience is the place where a believer's silent conversation is "Thank you, Lord"; when their midnight cry in praise is "Thank you, Lord"; when God allows the believer's faith to be challenged and he makes a way out of no way, the believer's narrative is "Thank you, Lord." The believer's outpour of gratitude is expressed when believers are asked how they made it through their trials, believers are not afraid to mention that Jesus is their source of counsel.

This is a place where believers consider having one-on-one time with Jesus (the word of God) and enjoy every moment as they draw near him through the gifts of the Holy Spirit while the proof of the outpouring of the living water is being observed by an untold audience. The word of God (Jesus) becomes alive in the believers so much so that their passion to share the good news of Jesus is clearly seen because of the living water present in all the believer does. This is the place where Jesus becomes the believer's friend, companion, confidant, comrade, compadre, helpmate, and the great I am.

The Fountain Gate is the place where believers return to evangelizing with the power of God (gospel), with tangible and intangible evidence. The idea that believers unconsciously spill their truths to anyone who will listen with strong confidence defines and demonstrates a well of living waters. This overflow of fullness continues in the form of service to people toward those God has placed in the believer's care for spiritual counseling.

There is a sharing attitude propelled by the filling

of the Holy Spirit when sowing the word of God. The word of God is a designated food source that causes a change in the life of mankind. There is an evangelistic compassion that flows out of the heart of the believer toward mankind as they consecrate themselves to the will of God.

This is the place and time the spiritual gifts from God, associated with the filling of the Holy Spirit, identify which gift(s) is aligned with the believer's purpose. The believer's resiliency and rigidity regarding this gift of the filling of the Holy Spirit will be put into its proper perspective with obedience in the watergate to the prompting of the Holy Spirit.

Application

Have you been filled with the power of the Holy Spirit? Has the word of God poured out of your spirit unconsciously? Do you have a spiritual song or hymn in your heart that your spirit sings without ceasing, without consciousness?

I recommend spending some one-on-one time in God's word. The Holy Spirit's purpose in the believer's life is tied to the word of God. Believers are charged to come to the Fountain Gate for living water daily.

Acknowledgments

I take no credit for this book's content and wisdom expressed in these pages of illuminating living water. These saying are given by the inspiration of God for the edification of those God has prepared to take hold. I thank my God, my Lord, Savior Jesus Christ, and the Holy Spirit for this great commission to tell the stories of God's reconciliation and salvation plan for mankind.

I thank my parents, Mr. Jessie Riley and Mrs. Dinah Mae Riley, for their constant chasing and chastising me with love that brought me to this place of faith.

There are many people to who I'm thankful for their inspiration and motivation to write this book. To my incredible wife, Mrs. Marilyn Riley. Without her loving, giving, and supporting spirit, this book would not be possible. To my daughters, Shannett and Tennisha Riley, you are truly a blessing from God. Thank you for your inspiration and constant encouragement to continue the fight to finish this book. Only God loves you more.

Thanks to my neighbor, friend, and author of several books, Mr. Skip Johnson. Skip, your confidence in my abilities and the many gifts define you as a spiritual midwife and a benefactor in my life sent by God.

Thanks to my editor, brother in Christ, and friend,

Mr. Joseph Brassfield. Joseph, many thanks for the fellowship, strength, motivation, and spiritual guidance that you provided while editing this book. Your gifts and talents exposed in this book cannot be measured. You are my confidant in Christ Jesus.

About the Author

The author, Ralph Riley, is one of eight boys born to parents of sharecroppers in a small Florida town. His parents held unwavering faith and diligence while working hard to provide the necessities of life for their family.

The content of this book impregnated him long ago but didn't make haste to release its wisdom. He is grateful and beholden that God would use him to reveal his power over all the power of the enemy.

www.ingramcontent.com/pod-product-compliance
Lightning Source LLC
Chambersburg PA
CBHW071251070526
44583CB00017B/2423